D1007812

THE POWER OF
meow

Also by Bernard Gunther

Energy Ecstasy
Sense Relaxation
What to Do till the Messiah Comes
How the West Is One
The One Minute Enlightenment
New Sage Cards
Fast Food for the Soul
49 Flavors of Love

Energy Meditation CD
The Enlightenment CD

THE POWER OF
meow

from rumi to me

BERNARD GUNTHER

HAMPTON ROADS
PUBLISHING COMPANY, INC.

for the evolving human spirit

Copyright © 2006 by Bernard Gunther

Cover design by Jane Hagaman
Cover and interior photos by Jay Calis

Hampton Roads Publishing Company, Inc.
1125 Stoney Ridge Road
Charlottesville, VA 22902
434-296-2772
fax: 434-296-5096
e-mail: hrpc@hrpub.com
www.hrpub.com

If you are unable to order this book from your local
bookseller, you may order directly from the publisher.
Call 1-800-766-8009, toll-free.

Library of Congress Cataloging-in-Publication Data

Gunther, Bernard.
  The power of meow / Bernard Gunther.
      p. cm.
  Summary: "Spiritual teacher Bernard Gunther celebrates the mystical essence and
inherent wisdom of our feline companions. Gunther offers a series of "awareness
reminders" inspired by his own cat Rumi and reinforces the message that staying in
the moment is the key to happiness"--Provided by publisher.
  ISBN 1-57174-477-0 (5 1/2 x 6 1/2 tp : alk. paper) 1. Cats--Religious aspects. 2.
Spiritual life. I. Title.
  BL443.C3G86 2006
  202'.12--dc22

                          2005034605

ISBN 978-1-57174-477-7

10 9 8 7 6 5 4 3 2

Printed on acid-free paper in Canada

acknowledgments

multi much thanks
and grateful appreciation to:
kathryn hall
bill gladstone ming russell
j. e. williams
josh kransoff stephanie faillers
irv katz randy tadai
del weston tim lynch rick benzel
judith & bruce reno
rick & jan petok
rabbi robby gordon mark ralston
bobby disalvio
jane hagaman ross howell
for the marvelous photos
by jay calis
and my mischievous master
rumi

for the one
superconscious soul
in the form of
eckhart tolle

"I have known
three zen masters
in my life
and all of them
were cats."
—eckhart tolle

zen is
nothing special

doing one thing
at a time

no subject
no object
no problem

introduction

it had been
for no reason
a long time
since i lived with a cat

i love them
their furry softness
alert presence
regal grace
awareness aloofness
independent bliss
take you for grantedness

anyway i was ready
but knowing it's better
to let a cat come
than to choose one
i let it be known that
i wanted a cat
and open waited

fairly soon
a friend told me
she had found
the perfect cat for me

she was right
it was delight
at first sight
and he went
to bed with me
the very first night

when rumi
first arrived
his name was gatsby
gatsby fitzgerald
it obviously
didn't fit him
he was no gatsby
who was into
disappointment
and tragedy
while this cat
seemed calm
contemplative
in confident harmony
what to call him

it soon became clear
that he was
a deeply
spiritual being
and the name
rumi came
rumi was a sufi mystic
a magnificent poet
a master teacher
who knew the
divine mystery
deeply completely

the book that follows
are the teachings
of this rare aware cat
from rumi to me

the power of meow

is fully being
at this moment

completely present
totally aware
your boundless
real authentic

cat like nature

rumi is my roommate
we've been together
for almost a year
he's half siamese
half human
super fur fine white
orange sherbet ears and tail
eyes open wise
licking himself
he intuitively seems to go
to those places
i least want him to be
and he lets me know
when he's hungry
needs attention
when he wants to be groomed
or is going to toss up a hair ball
or when he wants me
to chase him around the bed
so he can rationalize
hiding under the covers
and taking a long nap
but he comes to me
whenever i call him
if he feels like it
and he only bites me softly
when we play

plus the whole night through
he quietly sleeps next to me
and we understand love
each other beyond words
and all in all it's by far
the very best intimate relationship
i've ever had

true love
is being in love
with the ultimate
source of love

life is like a cat
in that
it often doesn't do
what you want it to
it tests annoys
frustrates fascinates
exacerbates
sometimes confuses you

spontaneous demanding
amusing free
life is not your fantasy
it is what's true
what's ultimately
good for you
because all in all
it's your spiritual teacher
your guru

when you learn
to deal
with what is
not ideal
your life
will be
a good deal
easier

he's
a mouse
a rabbit
a hobbit
a habit

an aware bear
fred astaire

a lover
a tiger
a silly goose
a papoose

a pet
a buddha pest
the beast best
of all the rest
east and west

he's my purrfect
zen master
roshi rabbi rumi

we are all
shades and colors
of the
incandescent glow
of love's everlasting
dancing rainbow

at each
and every moment
roshi rumi
naturally
effortlessly
lives the dharma

without
having read
alan watts
gautama buddha
or bodhidharma

in reality
spirituality
is not about
glamour intensity
or escapist meditation
but about being
fully present
in every
moment to moment
relationship and situation

adept rumi
is a superb sleeper

rather than hurrying
worrying or
yap yap yapping
he's deeply
into napping

choosing sneezing
if there's nothing
better to do
he can sleep
anywhere
often where
you don't
want him to

for example
just now
he decided to flop
right on my
laptop

you don't
have to prove
or improve yourself
all you have to do
is approve
of yourself

there are times
when master rumi
reminds
me of my mind
he seems restless
demanding
dissatisfied
makes lots of anoise
and i can't tell
what the hell
he really wants

though right now
he's sitting
serene still

without content

he is completely

content

let all
thinking
cease

and you are

peace

mostly
rumi just sits
observing
the passing flow
watching as
all things
come and go

nonattached
unbiased
awareness

a witness fair

accepting
adjusting
reacting
to what is
intuitively
knowing
it's all just
show biz

if you don't stay
in your awareness
witness consciousness
reality

you will
fall into
do do ality

in every now
rumi practices
the tao

sitting quietly
doing nothing
food comes
and the litter box
magically
empties
itself

if the sun
and the moon
were to doubt
all the love magic
that is all about
they would both
go out

no doubt

shree rumi
is not dependent
on excitement
intensity or
constant doingness

he is beingness
consciousness
alert aliveness
living in
moment to moment
awareness

and doing his business

it's enough
to be alive
to see the sea
the sky
and watch
the changes
to eat talk
joke serve and create
love feel
the air ground
sun yourself
and not
have to be
somebody

rumi
is also a sufi

understanding
the changing dance
of impermanence
he does not cling
to anything
knowing that
every thing
is very
temporary

he just watches
the passing flow
letting things
come and go

undivided
nonresisting
nonattached

he be

head to totally

free

go look
somewhere else
for subject matter
for what does
the subject matter
for all matter
is subject to
other matter
and it really
ultimately
doesn't matter

swami rumi
is a yogi

always
stretching
yawning
breathing
meditating
in harmony

he is unity
the infinite
formless
no one

playing form
fur fun

don't take
the game
too seriously
stay laugh play
in delight

rumi
not only
likes himself
he licks himself

every day
he works away
spring cleaning
his furry body

it's a contemplative joy
to the point of cheers
watching him
gently intensely
washing his face
and behind his ears

after he seems delighted
elated rejuvenated

it's the paws
that refreshes

love yourself
for no one
can be closer
or share more time
with you

be patient
and kind to yourself

value your attainments
appreciate your gifts

let go of the past
retaining only
its wisdom

remain aware
for you are now

new

when rumi
is hungry
he cries loudly
like a baby
wanting his
needs met
immediately

then patiently
he looks smells
tastes to see
if what is
available
is gourmet
worthy

patience
if given a chance
can enhance
the soul's dance
to advance

rumi san
is a being
of action
reaction
satisfaction

without guilt
excessive desire
or contraction

a consciousness
awareness glow
with no
past future
thinking ego

no self
no problem

only cathartic glee

empty empty
happy happy

when you identify
with the past
ego desire mind
you get stuck
in the behind

one of the places
that rumi loves best
is lying on my chest

first thing
in the morning
he settles there
purring like
a finely tuned porsche

mostly
i wake feeling
very blessed
but sometimes
i need my rest
and all i want to do
is get him
off my chest

it's not
what happens
but what you
tell yourself
that makes things
awful
good
or bad

reverend rumi
is an all-coholic

lovingly addicted
to the process
of life

meowing at what
he wants to change
eventually accepting
what he can't change

and not
taking it
personally
seriously

or catastrophically

if you make a mistake
make it a take
learn from it
don't dwell on it
forgive yourself
and move on

some people suffer
just for the
hell of it

one day
mystic rumi
went away

it was sad
too bad
but what
to do

after ten days
and nights
i gave up
ever seeing
him again

on the morning
of the eleventh day
he showed up
lean and hungry
with no explanation
or apology
feed me

for two days
he ate and slept

since then
he stays
close to home
appreciating
how good
he's got it

value
what you have
as much as
what you want

rabbi rumi
searches and researches
the yard each day

seeing smelling hearing
touching tasting
somehow
the fresh new meow
of every present

flowing knowing
that before original sin
there is intense
subtle immense

original innocence

the wonderful
wondrous world
beyond words
is right here
in front of you

shaman rumi
being always there
does not have to
achieve anything
or get anywhere

spontaneous free
with no obsession
tragic story
or chronic fear
or anxiety
life is a constantly
unfolding joyful
playful mystery

liberated he
is beyond all
category

every moment
thought feeling
experience situation
is an opportunity
for greater awareness
consciousness and
transformation

cats
they
take over
defy
sit lie
wherever
they want to
expecting
demanding
to be fed
petted groomed
doomed
you have to
clean their box
every day
while they sleep
more than half
the day away

what a stiff
price to pay
just for a little
pussy
cat

taking care
of everyone
includes
you

someday
beloved rumi's
physical body
will pass away
and he will be
sorely missed

yet we all know
that every form
is temporary
like momentary waves
on the surface
of the ocean
just a formation motion
that will dissolve
and return
into the ocean

so in ultimate reality
he me we
always are
have always been
and always will be
one in the sacred
essence sea
eternally
in unity

who you think you are
can't survive
who you really are
can't not survive

if there's
nothing to do
rumi does nothing

quietly
he sits waits
and meditates
silent empty
calm keen
fully absorbed
in the serene

christ awake aware
contracting and expanding
one in the peace
beyond all
understanding

you are
the awareness space
in which it all
takes place

all thinking
is dreaming
all thought
is pretend

be still
trans/end

we are all
melting
in the fire
of love's
ultimate desire

no you
no me
no rumi

be
mt

let go of the doer
and the doing
and you are
done

there's no you
or me
there's just
we
   e
    e
     e
      e
       e
        e
         e
          e
           e

meow
must
stay

rumi means namasté

i salute
the beingness
within you
that is divine